A Random House TELL ME ABOUT Book

OCEAN ANIMALS

By Michael Chinery
Illustrated by Eric Robson

Random House 🏠 New York

First American edition, 1992.

Copyright © 1991 by Grisewood & Dempsey Ltd.
All rights reserved under International and Pan-American
Copyright Conventions. Published in the United States by
Random House, Inc., New York. Originally published in Great
Britain by Kingfisher Books, a Grisewood & Dempsey Company,
in 1991.

Library of Congress Cataloging in Publication Data
Chinery, Michael.
Ocean animals / by Michael Chinery;
illustrated by Eric Robson.
p. cm. — (A Random House tell me about book)
Includes index.
Summary: Introduces animals of the oceans and how they live.
ISBN 0-679-82046-9   ISBN 0-679-92046-3 (lib. bdg.)
1. Marine fauna—Juvenile literature. [1. Marine animals.]
I. Robson, Eric, ill. II. Title. III. Series.
QL122.2.C55   1992
591.92—dc20
91-53144

Manufactured in Hong Kong 1 2 3 4 5 6 7 8 9 10

Contents

Life in the oceans

Thousands of different kinds of animals live in the oceans. Most of them live in the top 650 feet. Beneath this sunlit zone is the twilight zone, where there is not much light, but still plenty of fish and other creatures. Below 3,000 feet, the sea is completely dark and very cold. Some very odd fish live there, mostly with big mouths and sharp teeth.

 OCEAN FACTS

● We take millions of tons of fish from the oceans every year, and many species are in danger of being wiped out forever.

 **DO YOU KNOW**

The deepest water is in the Mariana Trench in the Pacific Ocean. It is 36,198 feet deep, but some creatures even manage to live there in the cold and the darkness. Mount Everest could sit on the bottom of the trench without breaking the surface.

THE WORLD'S OCEANS

Oceans and seas cover three quarters of the world's surface. Unlike lakes and rivers, oceans are saltwater. There are five oceans – the Pacific, the Atlantic, the Indian, the Arctic, and the Antarctic – plus several smaller seas. Water temperatures vary from one area to another. The Arctic Ocean, around the North Pole, is largely frozen over all year round.

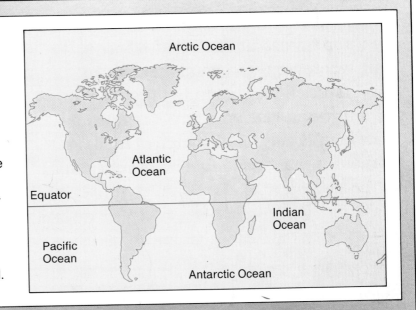

Arctic Ocean

Atlantic Ocean

Equator

Pacific Ocean

Indian Ocean

Antarctic Ocean

Drifting ocean life

The surface layers of the sea are full of plankton – small animals and plants that drift wherever the currents take them. Planktonic animals include tiny jellyfish, sea slugs, and many shrimp-like creatures. Plankton forms a vital source of food, and without it there would be no other animals in the sea.

 DO YOU KNOW

The purple sea snail makes an unsinkable raft by trapping air in the slime from its foot. The slime hardens and looks like plastic bubbles. The snail hangs from the raft and catches animals that bump into it.

The shrimp-like krill is only 2 inches long, but it is the main food of the blue whale and of many penguins.

Transparent, dart-like arrow worms, 1–4 inches long, attack other animals and kill them with sharp spines.

The sea gooseberry looks like a glass marble. It catches other animals with its long, sticky tentacles.

 PLANKTON FACTS

● Sea urchins and many other animals live at the surface only when they are young.

● Plankton is most common in cold seas.

This strange creature will eventually turn into a sea urchin – if it is not eaten by another animal first.

The bony herring

The herring is one of the most common fish in the sea. It lives near the surface in huge schools that may contain millions of fish. Each fish watches its neighbors, and they all swim in the same direction. They feed on small planktonic creatures. Herrings are eaten by bigger fish, and also by gulls and other seabirds. We catch herrings as well. They are very good to eat, although bony.

HERRING FISHING

Fishing boats catch millions of herrings every year. In some areas they have caught too many and the fish have almost died out.

The herring's scales get bigger every year. We can tell how old a herring is by looking at its scales.

The gills under this flap take oxygen from the water so the herring, like all fish, can breathe underwater.

The herring swims forward by waving its tail from side to side. The other fins help the fish to steer.

DO YOU KNOW

A female herring lays up to 50,000 tiny eggs. The eggs sink to the seabed, but the baby herrings swim to the surface soon after hatching. They can live for 25 years.

The huge blue whale

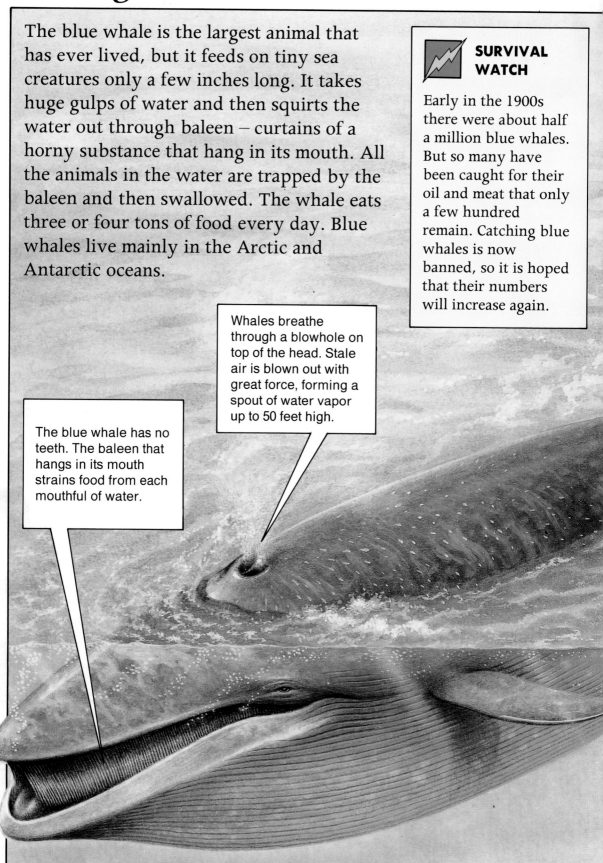

The blue whale is the largest animal that has ever lived, but it feeds on tiny sea creatures only a few inches long. It takes huge gulps of water and then squirts the water out through baleen – curtains of a horny substance that hang in its mouth. All the animals in the water are trapped by the baleen and then swallowed. The whale eats three or four tons of food every day. Blue whales live mainly in the Arctic and Antarctic oceans.

SURVIVAL WATCH

Early in the 1900s there were about half a million blue whales. But so many have been caught for their oil and meat that only a few hundred remain. Catching blue whales is now banned, so it is hoped that their numbers will increase again.

Whales breathe through a blowhole on top of the head. Stale air is blown out with great force, forming a spout of water vapor up to 50 feet high.

The blue whale has no teeth. The baleen that hangs in its mouth strains food from each mouthful of water.

The tail is like a huge flipper, about 23 feet across. It beats up and down and drives the whale at nearly 20 mph (miles per hour).

DO YOU KNOW

Whales are not fish. They are warm-blooded, air-breathing mammals. Their ancestors once had legs and lived on land.

Whales call to each other with sounds that travel many miles.

The baby is called a calf. Its mother pushes it to the surface as soon as it is born so that it can take its first breath of air.

BLUE WHALE FACTS

● The whale can hold its breath for over half an hour while diving.

● The blue whale may be up to 100 feet long and weigh up to 120 tons – as much as 25 elephants or 1,800 people.

Jellyfish

Jellyfish look like floating umbrellas. They have no brain and no skeleton. They swim jerkily by pumping water in and out of their bodies. Many have painful stings on their tentacles and use the stings to catch food. Some jellyfish are over 7 feet across.

This very common jellyfish, called the aurelia, often washes up on the shore. Up to about 20 inches across, it is easily recognized by the four purplish rings on top. It can sting but it is not dangerous.

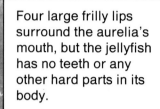

Four large frilly lips surround the aurelia's mouth, but the jellyfish has no teeth or any other hard parts in its body.

The aurelia has a sticky coat that traps tiny animals for food. The jellyfish licks them up with its lips, which then carry them up to its mouth.

A JELLYFISH GROWS UP

Jellyfish eggs do not grow straight into new jellyfish. The tiny creatures that hatch from the eggs settle on rocks or seaweeds and grow into what look like small sea anemones. These slowly divide until they look like piles of frilly saucers. Each "saucer" then breaks free and floats away to become a new jellyfish.

The Portuguese man-of-war

This strange-looking creature is a distant cousin of the jellyfish. It is really a colony of hundreds of little animals, all joined together under a sort of balloon that keeps them afloat. Each animal has its own job. Some catch food, others digest it, and others produce eggs. The stings on the man-of-war's tentacles can be very painful and dangerous.

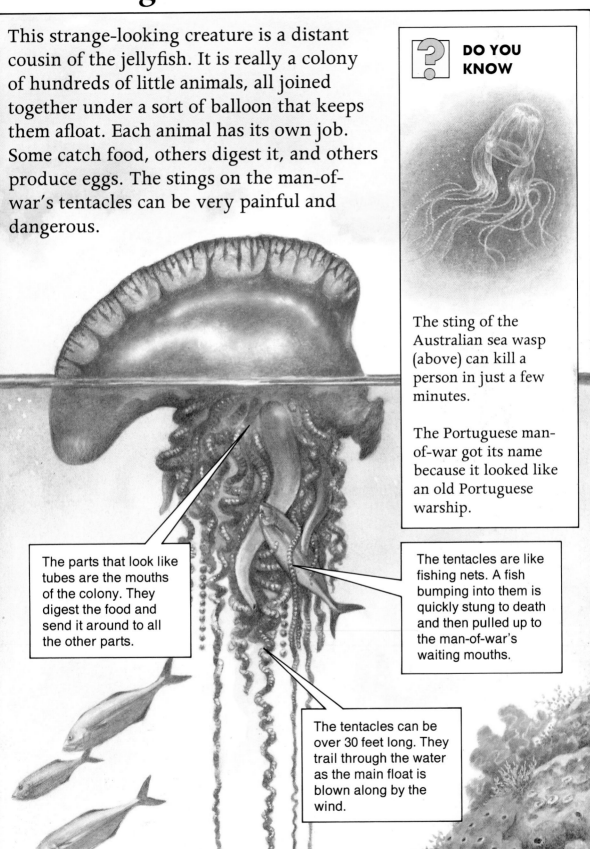

The sting of the Australian sea wasp (above) can kill a person in just a few minutes.

The Portuguese man-of-war got its name because it looked like an old Portuguese warship.

The parts that look like tubes are the mouths of the colony. They digest the food and send it around to all the other parts.

The tentacles are like fishing nets. A fish bumping into them is quickly stung to death and then pulled up to the man-of-war's waiting mouths.

The tentacles can be over 30 feet long. They trail through the water as the main float is blown along by the wind.

Fish that fly

Several kinds of fish are called flying fish, although none can really fly. They just leap out of the water and glide along on their fins for a while before crashing back into the water. The largest of these fish is the manta, which is shown here. It leaps high out of the water but never glides very far. It falls back with a tremendous splash.

MANTA FACTS

● The manta looks like a huge bat when it leaps from the water and is sometimes called the sea bat. It is also sometimes known as the devilfish.

● The manta is not a dangerous fish – as long as it doesn't fall on your boat! It feeds on small planktonic animals as it flaps slowly along just below the surface.

The fins of the manta can be more than 20 feet across, and the fish can weigh up to 4,500 pounds.

The manta gets the name devilfish from the horn-like flaps on its head. The horns scoop food into its mouth.

SMALLER FLYING FISH

The smaller flying fish probably leap into the air as a fast way of avoiding their enemies.

Driven by its tail, the fish swims rapidly toward the surface with its fins held close to its sides.

Breaking the surface, the fish spreads its fins. A few more flicks of its tail and it is airborne.

Flights can last for over half a minute and carry the fish several hundred feet through the air.

The jet-propelled squid

The squid is one of the fastest animals in the sea. It sucks water into its body and then squirts it out through a narrow tube. The force of the jet shoots the squid through the water at up to 35 mph. It can move both forward and backward. Squid eat fish and other animals, which they catch with their ten sucker-covered tentacles.

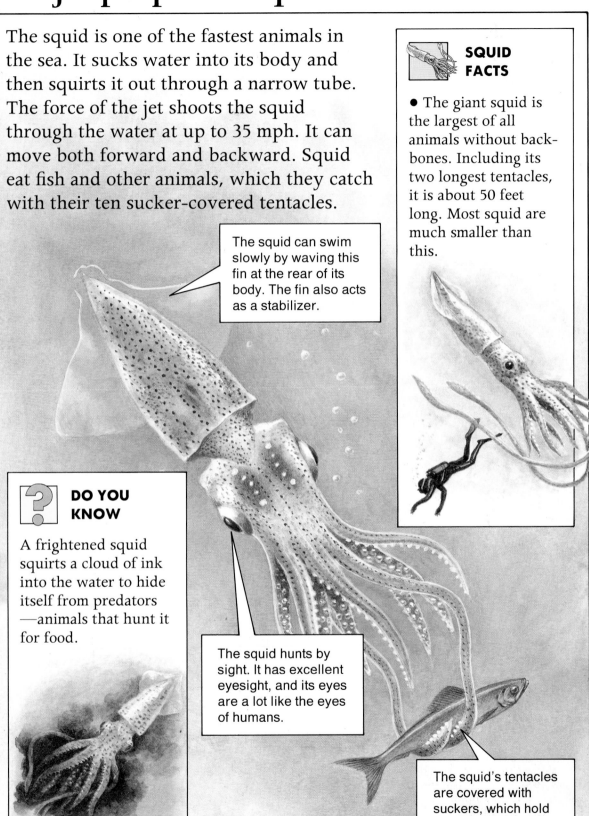

SQUID FACTS

● The giant squid is the largest of all animals without back-bones. Including its two longest tentacles, it is about 50 feet long. Most squid are much smaller than this.

The squid can swim slowly by waving this fin at the rear of its body. The fin also acts as a stabilizer.

DO YOU KNOW

A frightened squid squirts a cloud of ink into the water to hide itself from predators —animals that hunt it for food.

The squid hunts by sight. It has excellent eyesight, and its eyes are a lot like the eyes of humans.

The squid's tentacles are covered with suckers, which hold the prey firmly while the squid bites it.

Sharks – terrors of the sea

Sharks are among the most dangerous fish in the sea. Some of the bigger kinds, like the great white shark pictured here, are called man-eaters. They don't often attack swimmers, but when they do, their razor-sharp teeth can cause terrible injuries. Most sharks eat other fish; the huge whale shark, however, feeds only on tiny plankton, just like the blue whale. Some of the smaller sharks are called dogfish. Most sharks give birth to live babies, but some lay eggs inside tough cases.

 DO YOU KNOW

Sharks have no bones. Their skeletons are made of a soft material called cartilage.

Shark skins are covered with rough scales. Fishermen once used the skins to scrub ship decks.

Pilot fish often swim with sharks. People once thought they guided the sharks, but they are really waiting for the sharks to drop scraps of food.

A shark's tail is large and powerful. Side-to-side movements of the tail drive the shark forward at speeds of up to 40 mph.

SHARK FACTS

● There are about 250 different kinds of shark. The smallest is just 6 inches long.

● The whale shark is the world's biggest fish. It can measure up to 50 feet long.

Whale shark

● A whale shark's skin is 8 inches thick, and its egg is bigger than a football.

The jaws have several rows of sharp teeth. When the front teeth wear out, the next row moves forward to take their place.

? DO YOU KNOW

Some sharks lay their eggs in cases which become tangled with seaweeds. The egg cases of some of the smaller sharks, like this dogfish, are called mermaid's purses. You can often find empty ones on the beach.

Egg cases

Egg

Baby dogfish

The big front fins act like aircraft wings and help to lift the shark as it swims. They are also used for steering and braking.

The curious sawfish

The sawfish uses its strange snout to hit and wound other fish, and then snaps them up in its mouth. It also rakes small animals from the seabed with its snout. Sawfish live mainly in warm, shallow seas.

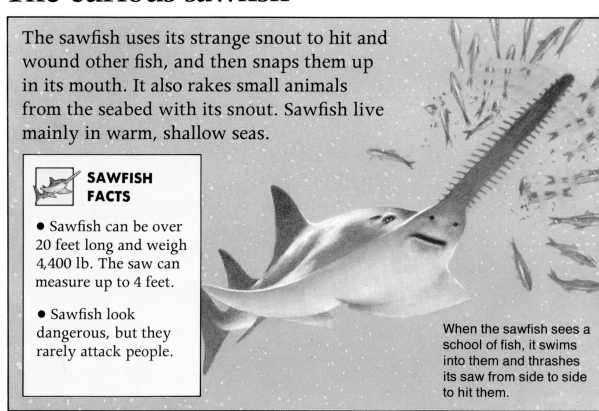

SAWFISH FACTS

• Sawfish can be over 20 feet long and weigh 4,400 lb. The saw can measure up to 4 feet.

• Sawfish look dangerous, but they rarely attack people.

When the sawfish sees a school of fish, it swims into them and thrashes its saw from side to side to hit them.

The speedy swordfish

The swordfish is one of the fastest fish in the sea. It can reach 60 mph in short bursts. It lives near the surface and uses its sword-like upper jaw to swat and injure smaller fish. It does not spear them.

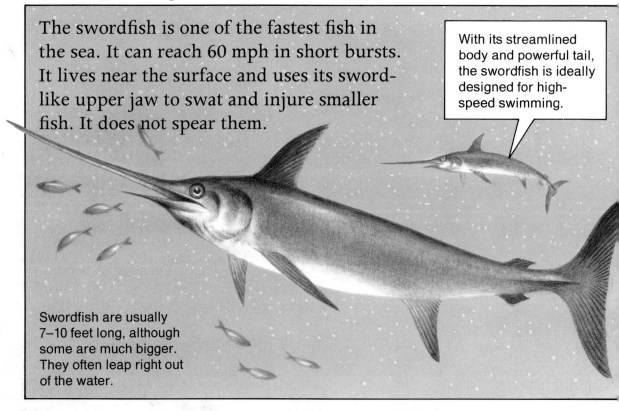

With its streamlined body and powerful tail, the swordfish is ideally designed for high-speed swimming.

Swordfish are usually 7–10 feet long, although some are much bigger. They often leap right out of the water.

The cod – a fine food fish

Cod like cold water and live mainly in the northern seas, including the Arctic Ocean. They usually live in fairly shallow water and often swim close to the shore. The cod has a huge appetite and catches many other fish, including herrings. It also eats squid and crabs. Cod can reach lengths of 5 feet or more, but most of those caught by fishing boats are 1–3 feet long.

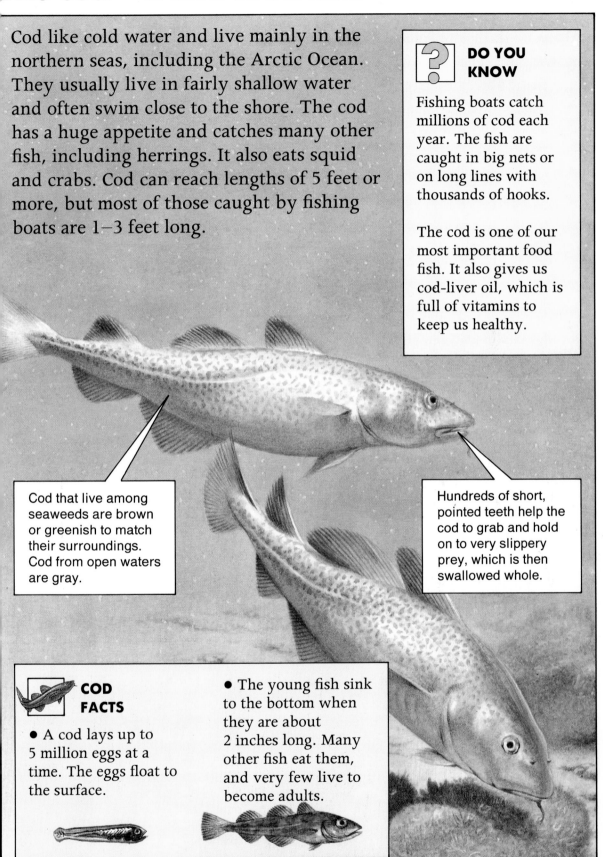

? DO YOU KNOW

Fishing boats catch millions of cod each year. The fish are caught in big nets or on long lines with thousands of hooks.

The cod is one of our most important food fish. It also gives us cod-liver oil, which is full of vitamins to keep us healthy.

Cod that live among seaweeds are brown or greenish to match their surroundings. Cod from open waters are gray.

Hundreds of short, pointed teeth help the cod to grab and hold on to very slippery prey, which is then swallowed whole.

COD FACTS

● A cod lays up to 5 million eggs at a time. The eggs float to the surface.

● The young fish sink to the bottom when they are about 2 inches long. Many other fish eat them, and very few live to become adults.

Intelligent dolphins

Dolphins are streamlined like fish and spend all their lives in the water, but they are not fish. They are air-breathing mammals and are actually small cousins of the whales. They are very intelligent animals, and scientists have learned that they talk to each other with a wide range of clicks, grunts, and whistles.

These bottle-nosed dolphins live in the Atlantic Ocean and the Mediterranean Sea. They can leap up to 30 feet out of the water.

 DO YOU KNOW

Dolphins are quick to learn and can be easily taught to do tricks in captivity. But many people think it is wrong to keep dolphins in this way, and many dolphins are being returned to the sea. Bottle-nosed dolphins are the most common ones in captivity.

The dolphin breathes through its blowhole when it comes to the surface. It also makes many different sounds through the blowhole while under the water.

The dolphin's tail beats up and down to drive it along through the water. Dolphins often leap high out of the water for the sheer fun of it.

DOLPHIN FACTS

Although they have small eyes, dolphins can actually see quite well. Even so, they rely mainly on their superb hearing to find their way around.

● The bottle-nosed dolphin always seems to be smiling due to the shape of its head.

● The dolphin's peg-like teeth give a good grip on the fish and squid on which it feeds.

THE KILLER WHALE

Like other dolphins, killer whales are kept in captivity and can be trained to perform various tricks.

The killer whale is really a large dolphin. Males reach lengths of about 30 feet. The animals hunt in packs and will often attack much bigger whales, although they prefer to eat seals, penguins, and fish.

The sperm whale – champion diver

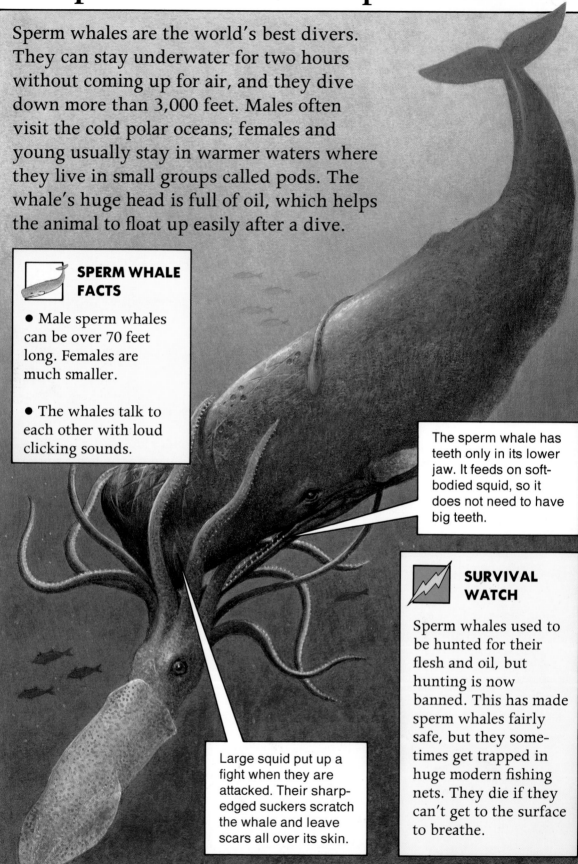

Sperm whales are the world's best divers. They can stay underwater for two hours without coming up for air, and they dive down more than 3,000 feet. Males often visit the cold polar oceans; females and young usually stay in warmer waters where they live in small groups called pods. The whale's huge head is full of oil, which helps the animal to float up easily after a dive.

SPERM WHALE FACTS

- Male sperm whales can be over 70 feet long. Females are much smaller.

- The whales talk to each other with loud clicking sounds.

The sperm whale has teeth only in its lower jaw. It feeds on soft-bodied squid, so it does not need to have big teeth.

SURVIVAL WATCH

Sperm whales used to be hunted for their flesh and oil, but hunting is now banned. This has made sperm whales fairly safe, but they sometimes get trapped in huge modern fishing nets. They die if they can't get to the surface to breathe.

Large squid put up a fight when they are attacked. Their sharp-edged suckers scratch the whale and leave scars all over its skin.

Bigmouthed gulper eels

The gulper eel looks like a terrible sea monster, but it is only 3–6 feet long. With its enormous mouth and elastic stomach, the gulper can swallow fish and other creatures bigger than itself. It lives in permanent darkness deep down in the sea.

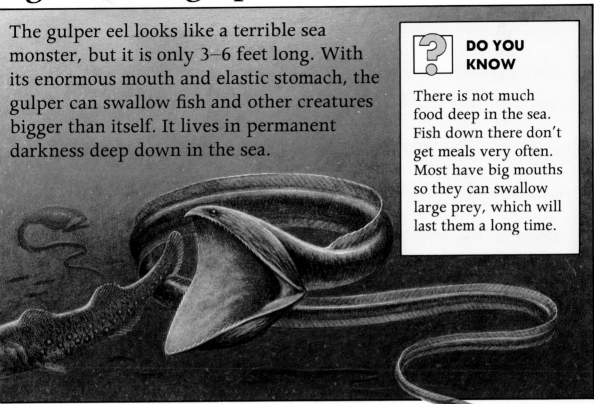

Fish with headlights

The fish in this picture (*pachystomius*) has an unusual way of finding food in the sunless waters of the deep sea. It has its own headlights, which send out a beam of red light that allows it to see other fish swimming in the surrounding water.

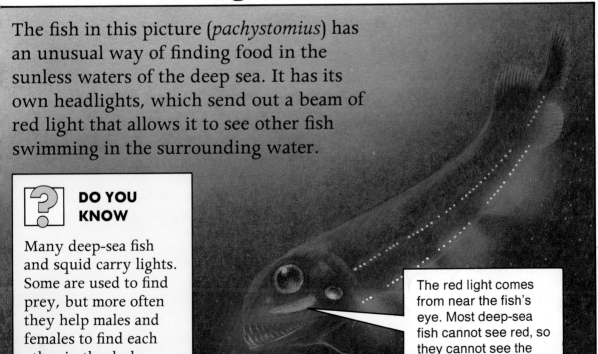

The red light comes from near the fish's eye. Most deep-sea fish cannot see red, so they cannot see the predator approaching.

The angler – a fish that goes fishing

The fierce-looking anglerfish pictured here live on the seabed along the coasts of Europe. They are up to 5 feet long. They wait for food to come to them and don't move very often. The front part of the top fin forms a fishing rod, and a little flap of skin on the end of it acts as bait. Smaller fish that come to the bait are snapped up.

DO YOU KNOW

Anglerfish weigh up to 90 pounds. Many tons are caught for food every year.

Female anglerfish can lay over a million eggs each year. The eggs float in long ribbons.

1. A small fish comes to investigate the bait waving around on the fishing rod above the angler's head.

2. The angler slowly lowers the bait toward its mouth, and the small fish follows it down.

DEEP-SEA ANGLERS

This strange-looking fish is one of many types of angling fish that live in total darkness deep in the ocean. This creature's shrimp-like bait has a red glow and attracts other fish right up to its mouth.

3. The angler opens its huge mouth and water rushes inside, carrying the small, helpless fish with it.

Lumbering lobsters

Lobsters belong to the large group of animals called crustaceans. They live in cool seas, usually close to the coast, where the seabed is rocky. Lobsters feed at night on all kinds of living and dead animals, including other lobsters. Adults reach 30 inches in length and weigh up to 9 pounds. Their huge claws can easily cut through a person's finger.

SURVIVAL WATCH

Lobsters are a popular dish, and thousands of them are trapped each year. They are becoming rare, and most countries now limit the numbers that can be caught.

Baby lobsters, called larvae, swim freely in the sea for about two weeks. Then they sink to the seabed.

DO YOU KNOW

Lobsters are caught in cages called lobster pots, which are baited with dead fish. As the picture shows, the animals are dark blue when they are alive, but they turn red when they are cooked.

The lobster can shoot backward through the water by flicking its broad tail fan forward like a flipper.

23

The octopus

Many people are terrified of octopuses, but these animals are not as dangerous as people think. Although some are over 20 feet across, most are much smaller. They lurk among rocks and dart out to catch shrimps and other small creatures. Like the squid, they move by jet propulsion (see page 13), but they can also crawl slowly on their eight arms. Octopuses are eaten by various large fish, which may first bite off their arms.

SURVIVAL WATCH

Octopuses are a popular food and are becoming rare in some areas because people catch too many of them. Polluted sea water is also causing them to die out in many places.

Water squirts out of this tube to push the octopus along. The tube can be aimed in any direction.

The octopus is often hard to see because it can change color to match different types of seabed.

The octopus has a horny beak between its eight arms. The beak is strong enough to crack open a crab's shell.

Color-changing cuttlefish

The cuttlefish is a distant cousin of the octopus, but it has ten arms, like the squid. It can shoot quickly backward by squirting water out through a kind of funnel. It can also shoot forward to snatch a shrimp or other prey. Cuttlefish live on the seabed, mainly in shallow coastal waters. They are even better at changing color than octopuses and can alter their appearance completely in less than a second.

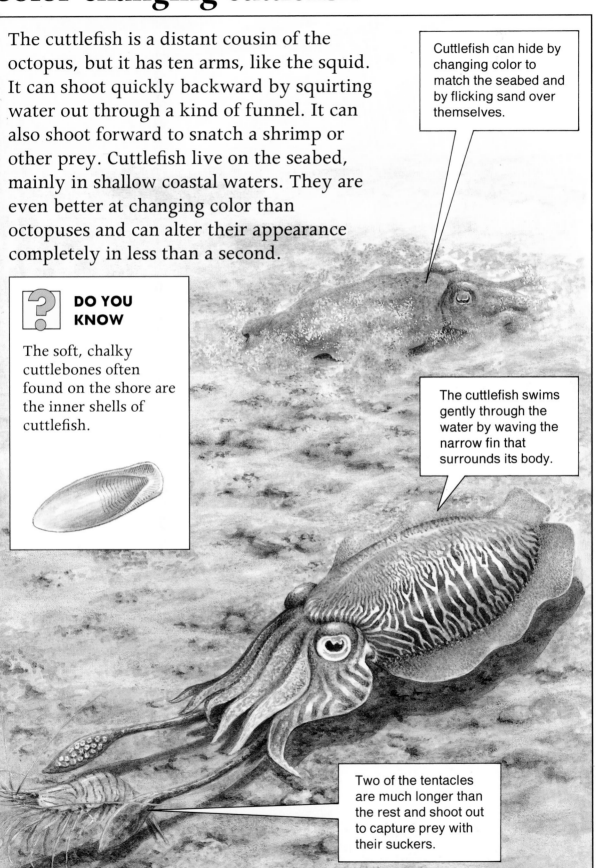

Cuttlefish can hide by changing color to match the seabed and by flicking sand over themselves.

? DO YOU KNOW

The soft, chalky cuttlebones often found on the shore are the inner shells of cuttlefish.

The cuttlefish swims gently through the water by waving the narrow fin that surrounds its body.

Two of the tentacles are much longer than the rest and shoot out to capture prey with their suckers.

The flat-bodied plaice

The plaice is a peculiar flat fish that lives on the seabed. Unlike the rays on the next page, it always lies on one side instead of on its belly. It almost always lies on its left side. It lives in coastal waters and feeds mainly on worms and thin-shelled shellfish. The plaice is an important food source, and fishing boats catch thousands of tons every year. Most of the fish that are caught are about 10–16 inches long.

A plaice can change color to match various parts of the seabed. It looks at the surroundings, and the color cells in its skin then shrink or swell to change its appearance. The plaice makes the camouflage complete by flicking sand and gravel over itself.

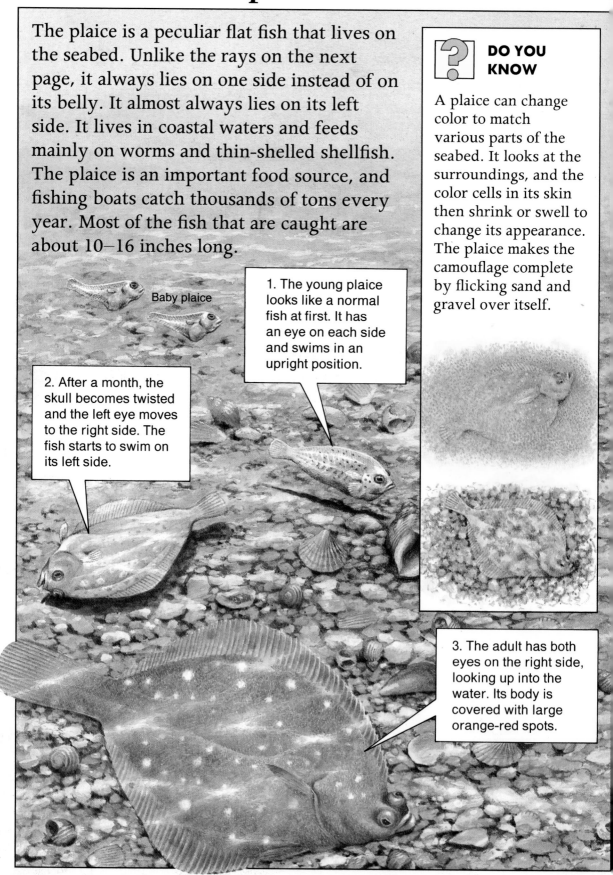

Baby plaice

1. The young plaice looks like a normal fish at first. It has an eye on each side and swims in an upright position.

2. After a month, the skull becomes twisted and the left eye moves to the right side. The fish starts to swim on its left side.

3. The adult has both eyes on the right side, looking up into the water. Its body is covered with large orange-red spots.

The torpedo – a shocking fish

Torpedos, or electric rays, stun their prey by sending electric shocks through the water. The dazed prey is then easily caught. A big torpedo, up to 7 feet long, can give a person a very bad electric shock.

The stingray

The stingray is a distant cousin of the torpedo. It gets its name from the poisonous spine on its long, whip-like tail. The fish lives mainly in shallow seas and feeds mostly on shellfish.

STINGRAY FACTS

• The spine is used for defense. It is up to 14 inches long and causes painful injury if it is stepped on.

• Stingrays grow to 8 feet in length.

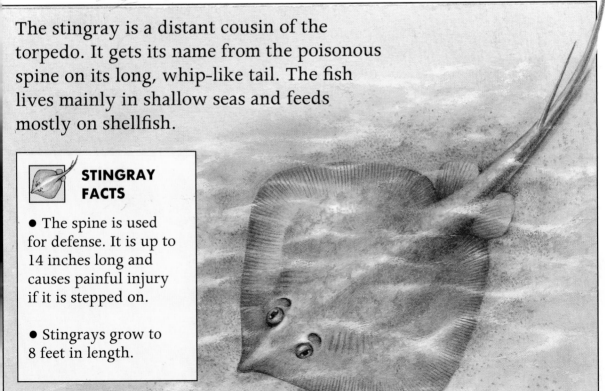

The coral reef

Coral reefs are like gardens under the sea. They are among the most colorful places on earth, but unlike ordinary gardens, they are not made up of plants. The corals themselves are tiny animals, and each one lives in a little chalky cup, which it builds itself. The corals cluster together and the cups form the coral rock; the living animals form a layer on the surface. Coral reefs are home to an amazing variety of fish and other animals.

The parrot fish eats coral. It snaps off pieces with its beak-like front teeth and crunches them up with its back teeth.

Sponges are simple animals that stay in one place. They feed by filtering tiny food particles from the seawater.

The sea anemone is a deadly trap for small fish and other animals. Its tentacles are covered all over with poisonous stings.

CORAL FACTS

- Corals are tiny relatives of sea anemones.

- In the daytime the animals retreat into their cups, and the coral looks like rock. At night they spread their tentacles to gather tiny planktonic creatures.

Reef-building corals live in clear, warm seas. The Great Barrier Reef, off the coast of Australia, is the largest of all reefs. Although built by animals the size of a pinhead, it forms a line of underwater hills 1,250 miles long.

Great Barrier Reef

AUSTRALIA

South Pacific Ocean

Antarctic Ocean

The conger is a large eel up to 10 feet long. It lurks between the corals and slithers out to catch fish in its strong, toothy jaws.

Angelfish are among the brightest of the coral reef fish. They are very thin and glide easily between the corals.

The crown of thorns is a large coral-eating starfish. It is rapidly destroying large areas of the Great Barrier Reef.

The giant clam weighs 600 pounds. Up to 3 feet across, it is one of the largest animals without a backbone.

Cleaners and barbers

A few fish have found some odd ways of getting their food. They have set themselves up as cleaners for larger fish. They are also known as barbers and often have special places where they wait for their customers to come for cleaning. They clean wounds and remove and eat dead skin and parasites from the larger fish.

DO YOU KNOW

Fish in search of cleaners look for their bright colors. But some fish, such as blennies, imitate the cleaners' colors. When customers arrive for a cleanup, the fake cleaners bite them instead.

Cleaner wrasse

Blenny

There are many kinds of cleaners in the world's seas. They often have bold black stripes. This one is a cleaner wrasse.

Barbers and cleaners often work inside the mouth of larger fish without harm. This one is cleaning the mouth of a grouper.

The strange sea horse

Sea horses are among the world's oddest fish. They don't really look like fish at all, and get their name because the head looks a little like a horse's head. They swim in an upright position but spend much of their time anchored to seaweeds. Another odd thing about sea horses is that the female lays her eggs in a pouch on the male's body and leaves him to look after them.

The sea horse's tiny mouth, at the end of its snout, snaps up tiny shrimp-like creatures for food.

 DO YOU KNOW

Sea horses don't look as if they are real animals. Their bodies have many bony ridges and appear to have been made from wood or plastic.

The fin on the back beats rapidly to push the sea horse forward. The fish simply turns its head to change direction.

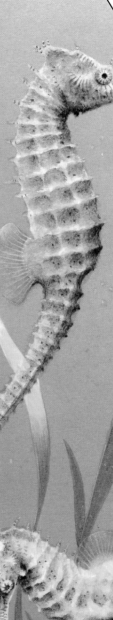

The male sea horse carries the eggs for four or five weeks and then gives birth to the babies. There may be 200 of them.

Sea horses anchor themselves to sea-weeds with their curly tails. They are often hard to see among the weeds.

Seals – super swimmers

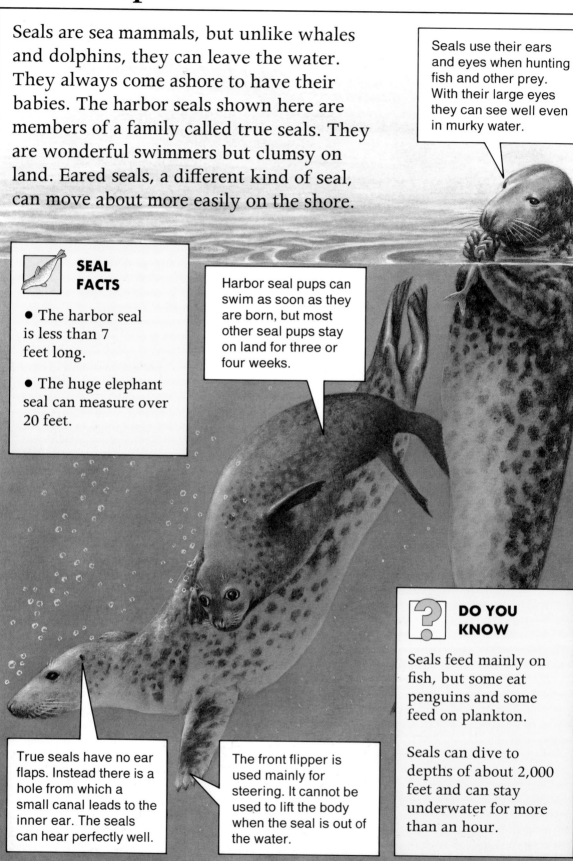

Seals are sea mammals, but unlike whales and dolphins, they can leave the water. They always come ashore to have their babies. The harbor seals shown here are members of a family called true seals. They are wonderful swimmers but clumsy on land. Eared seals, a different kind of seal, can move about more easily on the shore.

Seals use their ears and eyes when hunting fish and other prey. With their large eyes they can see well even in murky water.

SEAL FACTS

- The harbor seal is less than 7 feet long.

- The huge elephant seal can measure over 20 feet.

Harbor seal pups can swim as soon as they are born, but most other seal pups stay on land for three or four weeks.

DO YOU KNOW

Seals feed mainly on fish, but some eat penguins and some feed on plankton.

Seals can dive to depths of about 2,000 feet and can stay underwater for more than an hour.

True seals have no ear flaps. Instead there is a hole from which a small canal leads to the inner ear. The seals can hear perfectly well.

The front flipper is used mainly for steering. It cannot be used to lift the body when the seal is out of the water.

Playful sea lions

Sea lions look like true seals, but they have ear flaps and are more agile on land than true seals. Their flippers are bigger, and the front flippers can be used like legs. Sea lions live close to rocky coasts and spend a lot of time ashore. Males are much bigger than females. The sea lions shown here are California sea lions.

Sea lions have small ear flaps, but they can't hear any better than their relatives the true seals.

The back flippers can be turned forward and are used to push the sea lion along. They also do most of the steering when the animal is swimming.

In the water, the sea lion flaps its front flippers up and down like wings to drive it forward at high speed. It feeds mainly on fish and squid.

DO YOU KNOW

Sea lions have a wonderful sense of balance and can learn to perform amazing tricks. Some people think it is cruel to train animals to perform for people.

Dugongs – cows of the sea

The dugong is an unusual mammal. It spends all its life in the sea and looks like a seal, but it has no back legs. It is distantly related to horses and elephants and is the world's only vegetarian (plant-eating) sea mammal. Dugongs live along the coasts of the Indian and South Pacific oceans and graze on the meadows of sea grass that grow in the shallow waters. They can grow to 13 feet long and weigh up to 2,000 pounds.

DO YOU KNOW

The dugong probably started sailors' stories about mermaids. Floating with its head above the surface, it does look faintly human, but not much like a mermaid!

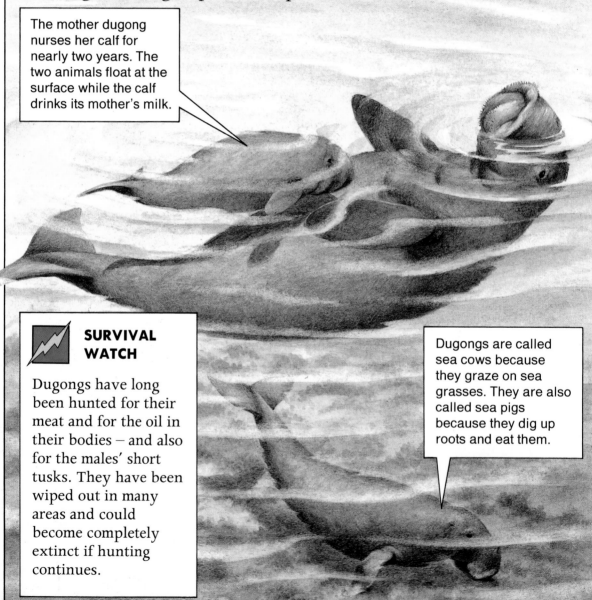

The mother dugong nurses her calf for nearly two years. The two animals float at the surface while the calf drinks its mother's milk.

SURVIVAL WATCH

Dugongs have long been hunted for their meat and for the oil in their bodies – and also for the males' short tusks. They have been wiped out in many areas and could become completely extinct if hunting continues.

Dugongs are called sea cows because they graze on sea grasses. They are also called sea pigs because they dig up roots and eat them.

Sea turtles

Turtles are sea-living tortoises. Their legs have become powerful flippers. The loggerhead turtle shown here lives in most of the warmer seas, including the Mediterranean. It eats seaweeds and all kinds of animals, such as prickly sea urchins and the deadly Portuguese man-of-war. It is unaffected by the man-of-war's poison.

SURVIVAL WATCH

Some sea turtles are in danger of dying out because people collect and eat their eggs. Tourism is another danger. Turtles lay their eggs only on particular beaches, and if these beaches become crowded with vacationers, the turtles will stay away.

Turtle shells are flatter and more streamlined than tortoise shells, making it easier for the animals to swim. The loggerhead's shell is up to 3 feet long.

The turtle's long front limbs flap up and down like the wings of a bird and drive the animal rapidly through the water.

Turtles spend almost all their lives at sea, but the females come ashore to lay their eggs, usually at night.

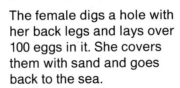

The female digs a hole with her back legs and lays over 100 eggs in it. She covers them with sand and goes back to the sea.

The eggs hatch in about nine weeks. The tiny turtles hurry down the beach, but many are caught by birds before they can reach the water.

The restless albatross

Albatrosses are long-winged seabirds about the size of geese. They glide and soar effortlessly over the waves for hours on end, seldom flapping their wings. Many albatrosses follow ships, and sailors often call them gooneys. Some birds stay out at sea for many years without ever coming to land, but they eventually come ashore to nest – usually in large colonies.

ALBATROSS FACTS

● The wandering albatross is the largest seabird. Its wings are nearly 13 feet across.

● Albatrosses pair up for life. Some pairs are known to have stayed together for over 30 years.

Long, narrow wings are ideal for soaring and gliding in the strong winds blowing over the open ocean.

The albatross uses its long beak to snatch fish and squid from the waves as it flies across the surface of the water.

DO YOU KNOW

Albatrosses nest on remote islands. The female lays one egg in a cup-shaped nest made with mud and grass. Some chicks are nine months old before they can fly. By then their parents are so exhausted, they need a year's rest before nesting again!

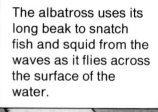

he frigate bird – ocean pirate

Frigate birds eat fish, but they don't always catch the fish themselves. They often chase other seabirds and make them give up any fish they have caught. This is why they are called pirates. Frigate birds fly only over the warmer seas of the world.

A frigate bird chases a tropical bird until the smaller bird drops the fish. The frigate bird will then swoop down to catch the fish.

The graceful gannet

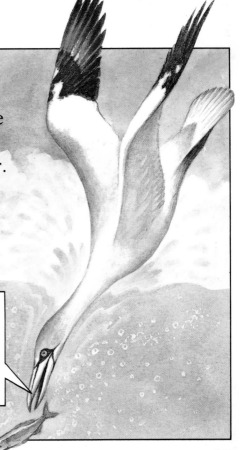

Gannets are superb divers. Flying about 100 feet above the sea, they dive at speeds of up to 100 mph when they see fish in the water. A gannet's skull is very thick, to withstand the crash when it hits the water.

SURVIVAL WATCH

Gannets nest on cliffs and small islands. Their numbers are increasing now that people have stopped taking their eggs for food.

Bony plates covering the gannet's nostrils stop water from getting up the bird's nose when it dives at full speed into the sea.

Oceans in danger

The oceans are huge, but they are rapidly being polluted by the waste material we dump in them. Tiny bacteria turn much of the waste into food for plankton, but they can't deal with poison from our factories. Traces of poison are found in fish all over the world, and they are also found in seabirds – and people – who eat the poisoned fish. If we are not careful, we will kill everything in the oceans and a lot of other animals as well.

Another danger to ocean life is fishing. Millions of tons of fish are caught every year in huge modern fishing nets. Fish numbers are now very low in some areas.

SAVING THE OCEANS

Most countries now ban the dumping of waste at sea. This includes the waste oil often dumped by ships. Oil clogs the feathers of seabirds and poisons them when they try to clean themselves. New laws are being introduced to increase the size of the holes in fishing nets. This is to allow small fish to escape so they can grow up and breed.

Useful words

Baleen The horny material forming the large curtain-like sheets that hang in the mouths of some whales and strain their food from the water. Baleen is also called whalebone.

Blowhole The nose or nostril of a whale or a dolphin, situated on the top of its head.

Camouflage The way in which animals avoid the attention of their enemies by blending in with their surroundings. The animals are then hard to see. Many animals use special patterns or colors as camouflage. Others change their appearance as their surroundings change. Some animals also use camouflage to trap their prey.

Coast The edge of the land, where it meets the sea.

Coastal Having to do with the coast. Coastal waters are those close to the coast.

Crustacean Any member of the lobster and crab group – hard-shelled animals with lots of legs.

Fin Any of the limbs or other flaps that fish use for swimming. The fins are often thin and delicate.

Flipper Any of the paddle-shaped limbs of marine mammals and turtles. Seals use them for steering and for forward movement. Whales use their flippers for steering and use their tails to drive them forward.

Mammal Any member of the large group of animals that feed their babies with milk from the mother's body.

Marine mammals include whales, seals, and dugongs. Most mammals have hair or fur, although whales are nearly hairless. All mammals breathe air.

Marine Having to do with the sea.

Parasite An animal that lives on or in another kind of animal and takes food from it without giving anything in return.

Plankton The floating mass of tiny plants and animals near the surface of the sea. The plankton is like a "living soup," and without it there would be no life in the ocean.

Pollution The poisoning of the ocean (or any other place) by oil or waste products from factories.

Predator Any animal that hunts or traps other animals for food.

Prey Any animal that is caught and eaten by a predator.

School The name commonly given to a large group of fish swimming together.

Shellfish The name given to various hard-shelled sea creatures, especially clams and mussels and their relatives. Crabs and other crustaceans are also commonly known as shellfish.

Tentacle A soft, finger-like projection near the mouth of many animals such as squid, octopuses, and jellyfish. Tentacles are mainly used for catching food.

Vegetarian An animal feeding only on plants.

Index